Hope
is a
Blanket

Printed in the United States of America
Published in Hellertown, PA
Cover and interior design by Leanne Coppola
Illustrated by Courtney Cuvo-Sanchez

Library of Congress Control Number available upon request.
ISBN 9781958711606

For more information or to place bulk orders, contact the author or the publisher at
Jennifer@BrightCommunications.net.

To our earthly and heavenly children,
and to everyone who has lost
someone they love.
May hope be what you find.

"Mama, please help me!
My blanket, I can't find it."
"My darling boy, don't worry,
Relax and stay calm-minded."

"It must be here,
Do not fear."

"I need it, or I cannot sleep.
I'll be up all night long,
No matter if we read a book,
And sing our goodnight song.

Blanket, blanket, where are you?
I just don't know what to do."

"Let's hope we find it very soon.
It's nearly time for bed."

"What does hope mean, Mama?"
the curious boy then said.

"I'll tell you about hope, my son,
As we search each room, one by one."

"Here in the playroom,
Big blanket forts we build.
We dream, play, and wrestle.
We feel safe, hearts are filled."

Hope is like a fortress,
Mighty and secure,
A rock in times of trouble,
A strength that is sure.

"Blanket's not here.
It must be near!"

"Here in the backyard,
We picnic in the sun,
Our blanket is our table,
For food, drinks, and fun."

Hope is a soft place,
To gather and to share,
To be nourished and be fed,
To give joy, love, and care.

"Blanket's not here.
It must be near!"

"Here in the den,
We play hide-and-seek.
Blanket is our cover,
A sneaky technique."

When life is sad or scary,
And we want to run and hide,
Hope can be a blanket,
Be our comfort, be our guide.

"Blanket's not here.
It must be near!"

"Here in the laundry room,
Blanket gets nice and clean,
Fluffs up in the dryer,
Comes out fit for a queen!"

Hope is a fresh start,
A future that is bright,
Anticipating goodness,
A world that is right.

"Blanket's not here.
It must be near!"

"Time's up my dear son,
Let's head up to bed.
We'll find blanket tomorrow,
Time to rest your sweet head."

Sometimes hope seems lost,
And life feels unfair,
Will it ever get better?
Does anybody care?

"Blanket, I need you!
Hope, I can't see you!"

"Let's get out some pjs,
From the top dresser drawer."
Tucked under some clothes,
Is what we've been searching for...

BLANKET!

"Blanket, you sure won
That game of hide-and-seek.
I forgot we were playing!
Let's try again...next week.

For now, it's time to rest,
And I know I finally can.
I knew we'd find you, blanket,
I had hope, again and again!"

"That's right, my cutie pie,
Hope was here all along!
Hope was the search, hope was blanket,
and hope is our goodnight song!"

"Hope is never lost
When it lives inside our hearts.
Hope is always with us,
To the end, and from the start."

"No matter where you go,
No matter what you do,
Hope is always just a couple
steps ahead of you.

Hope is like a blanket.
We long for its warm embrace,
Through the ups and downs of life,
As we grow in faith and grace."

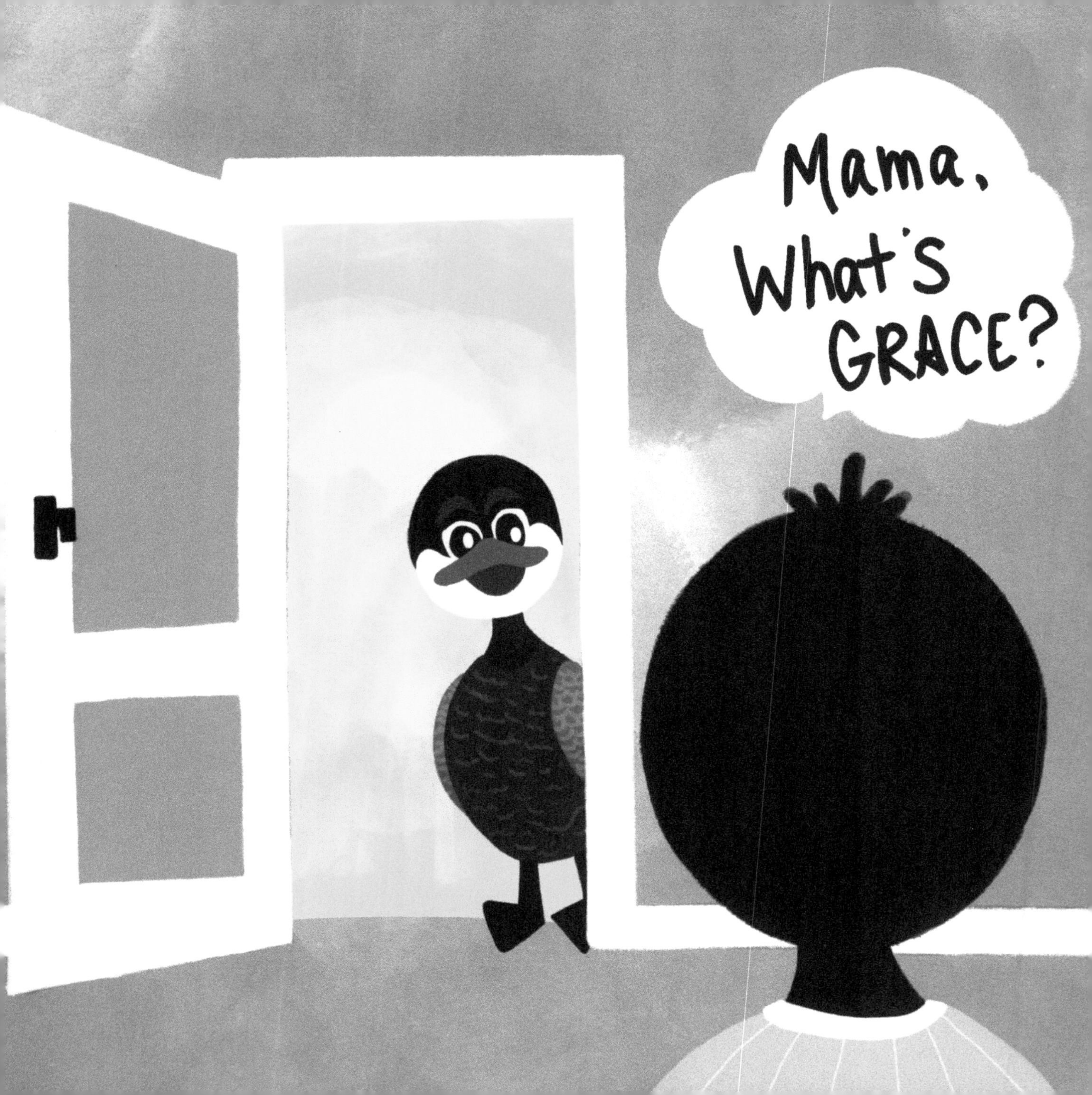
Mama, What's GRACE?

ACKNOWLEDGMENTS

Andrea

I raise my hands up to my Author, who made this story part of mine and continues to write the chapters of my life. Thank you to Courtney for taking a dream many years in the making and bringing it to life so beautifully. Jimmy, thank you for your enduring love and support - I don't know where I'd be without you. And Declan, your Saturday morning snuggles inspired this - I am so grateful you're my little wild goose.

Courtney

I would like to express my deepest appreciation to Andrea for trusting me enough to bring her vision to life; I am forever grateful for the opportunity to be involved in such an impactful book. Thank you to my closest friends, family, and husband - without your unconditional support and encouragement to try new endeavors, the images shown in this book would never have been possible.

Printed in the USA
CPSIA information can be obtained
at www.ICGtesting.com
CBHW080823080624
9695CB00005B/30

9 781958 711606